New Daylight

Three weeks of undated Bible reading

Text copyright © BRF 2003

Published by
The Bible Reading Fellowship
First Floor, Elsfield Hall
15–17 Elsfield Way, Oxford OX2 8FG
ISBN 1 84101 354 4

First published 2003
10 9 8 7 6 5 4 3 2 1 0
All rights reserved

Acknowledgments
Scripture quotations marked NRSV are taken from The New Revised Standard Version of the Bible, Anglicized Edition, copyright © 1989, 1995 by the Division of Christian Education of the National Council of the Churches of Christ in the USA, and are used by permission. All rights reserved.

Scripture quotations marked CEV are from the Contemporary English Version, published by The Bible Societies/HarperCollins Publishers, copyright © 1991, 1992, 1995 American Bible Society.

Scripture quotations marked NEB are from the New English Bible, copyright © 1961, 1970 by Oxford Univeristy Press and Cmbridge University Press.

A catalogue record for this book is available from the British Library

Printed and bound in Malta

CONTENTS

INTRODUCTION TO NEW DAYLIGHT

 The focus of our work here at BRF is helping people with Bible reading and prayer, as well as in understanding what it means to belong to the Christian Church. In reading the Bible, we learn more of how our faith fits together, and this can nurture our prayer life, both as individuals and as worshipping communities. Reading with the help of insightful comment from others can help us get more out of the Bible, challenge our assumptions, and bring us fresh insights into familiar passages.

This sampler offers three weeks of readings from our *New Daylight* notes, which provide a devotional approach to reading and understanding the Bible. Each issue of the notes covers four months of daily readings (with the Bible passage included) and reflection from a regular team of contributors from a wide range of church backgrounds. The readings selected here are by David Spriggs (The Holy Spirit), Veronica Zundel (The heart of the gospel) and Helen Julian CSF (Feasting and fasting).

I very much enjoy editing *New Daylight*, alongside my other BRF work of commissioning and editing our adult list as well as overseeing the publication of our other Bible reading notes. I hope that you will enjoy using the readings sampled here, and that they will inspire you to deepen your commitment to regular Bible study and prayer.

Naomi Starkey

Editor, *New Daylight*, and Managing Editor, Bible reading notes

NEW DAYLIGHT'S CURRENT TEAM OF CONTRIBUTORS

Rachel Boulding is Deputy Editor of the *Church Times*. For some years she was Senior Editor at SPCK Publishing.

Christine Chapman is currently a member of the North-West Inter-Diocesan Counselling Team for clergy and their families, and is a Reader in her church.

Margaret Cundiff has worked in the Church of England since 1973 as a lay worker, deaconess, deacon and finally priest. Her most recent book for BRF is *Still Time for Eternity* (2001).

Colin Evans is a former Moderator of the Eastern Province of the United Reformed Church, writer and broadcaster. He lives near Sudbury, in Suffolk.

Rob Gillion is Vicar of Upper Chelsea, London, and Evangelism Officer for the Bishop of Kensington. He was formerly a prison chaplain in Hong Kong.

Peter Graves is Minister of Wesley Church, Cambridge, and Chaplain to Methodist students at the University. He is the author of *Living and Praying the Lord's Prayer* (BRF 2002).

Helen Julian CSF is an Anglican Franciscan sister, a member of the Community of St Francis. She has written *Living the Gospel* for BRF (2001).

Adrian Plass is an internationally popular writer and speaker in many countries. His most recent book for BRF is *When You Walk*.

Jenny Robertson is based in Warsaw, Poland, where her husband is an Anglican Chaplain. Jenny has written *Strength of the Hills* and *Windows to Eternity* (both BRF, 2001 and 1999).

David Spriggs is a Baptist minister, currently working as Head of Church Relations for Bible Society, and author of *Feasting on God's Word* (BRF, 2002).

David Winter is an honorary Canon of Christ Church, Oxford, and is well known as a writer and broadcaster. He is the author of BRF's Advent book for 2003, *Hope in the Wilderness*.

Veronica Zundel is an Oxford graduate, writer and journalist. She belongs to the Mennonite Church.

The Spirit and servanthood

While everyone else was being baptized, Jesus himself was baptized. Then as he prayed, the sky opened up, and the Holy Spirit came down upon him in the form of a dove. A voice from heaven said, 'You are my own dear Son, and I am pleased with you.' … When Jesus returned from the River Jordan, the power of the Holy Spirit was with him, and the Spirit led him into the desert. For 40 days Jesus was tested by the devil.

The essential nature of Christian leadership is that it is servant leadership. This is the kind of leadership that Jesus chose for himself and it is the kind of leadership that he expects from his followers (John 13:1–20). It is not natural for leaders to behave like this, however, and it is in the nature of the power of leadership to corrupt.

At his baptism, Jesus received the Holy Spirit in a new and intense way. He also received confirmation that his ministry was one of service, which would ultimately lead to his death as a ransom for many (see Mark 10:45 and Philippians 2:1–11). His temptations show Jesus wrestling with and resisting various aspects of non-servant leadership and his sermon in Nazareth (Luke 4:18–27) shows his public declaration and commitment to the servant way. Throughout these episodes, Luke emphasizes the presence of the Spirit with Jesus (see 3:21–22; 4:1, 14, 18), because only with the empowering and sensitizing qualities of God's Spirit will Jesus keep on track. It is a very hard road to stay on.

Each of us leads—in the home if not at work; in the church if not at the WI; in some set of relationships if not as the captain of the team; on odd occasions if not by character. It is so important that we, like Jesus, lead with a servant heart, for it is a critical part of our witness for him. We certainly have no chance of success without the Holy Spirit's indwelling, but neither can we succeed without resisting the corruption that power can bring.

(For further reading, see Luke 4:1–30.)

Reflection

Imagine God sending his Holy Spirit on you like a dove, with all the challenges to lead like Jesus coming with it.

DS

Creative gifts

The Lord said to Moses: 'I have chosen Bezalel from the Judah tribe to make the sacred tent and its furnishings. Not only have I filled him with my Spirit, but I have given him wisdom and made him a skilled craftsman who can create objects of art with gold, silver, bronze, stone and wood. I have appointed Oholiab from the tribe of Dan to work with him.

In terms both of function and space devoted to it, the construction of the 'sacred tent' is clearly of great significance. It is where Moses and Aaron will meet with God and where sacrifices will be offered, enabling the covenant relationship to flourish. It is where Israel's sacred laws will be kept, indicating the centrality of these for her life as well as their divine origins. Above all, it is to be a place of worship, where God can meet his people and they can respond. So, although it is unusual, it is not surprising that the chief craftsman should be filled with God's Spirit—God tells Moses that he has 'filled him with my Spirit' and Moses tells the people the same (Exodus 31:3; 35:31).

As far as I know, Bezalel is the only craftsman to be designated in this way. It is important that creative and artistic skills are associated with God's Spirit. Wisdom, skilled craftsmanship, the ability to create objects of art with gold, silver, bronze, stone and wood are all mentioned, as are design and embroidery. We should celebrate these gifts and their creative achievements as indications of the creativity of God.

We should also recognize, however, that, according to scripture, the gift of God's Spirit is additional to these. Thus, Oholiab is closely associated with Bezalel in all his abilities, but is never said to have received God's Spirit. So the evidence of amazing creativity and artistic ability is not in itself synonymous with having God's Spirit! This is true even when the purpose is as significant a project as constructing the 'sacred tent'. (Nor, for that matter, is the ability to write, even Bible-reading notes, in itself evidence of God's Spirit!)

Prayer

Lord, help us to recognize and celebrate the origins of all creative abilities in you, but give us the discernment to know when these gifts are also flowing directly from your Spirit within us.

DS

Spiritual gifts

There are different kinds of spiritual gifts, but they all come from the same Spirit… The Spirit has given each of us a special way of serving others. Some of us can speak with wisdom, while others can speak with knowledge, but these gifts come from the same Spirit. To others the Spirit has given great faith or the power to heal the sick or the power to perform mighty miracles. Some of us are prophets, and some of us recognize when God's Spirit is present… But it is the Spirit who does all this and decides which gifts to give to each of us.

When we come to the New Testament, the range of people gifted with the Spirit, as well as the gifts themselves, suddenly opens out—rather than a river in a narrow channel, it now spreads out across the whole land (see Ezekiel 47:1–12; Revelation 22:1–2). Paul emphasizes that the variety of gifts is evidence of the richness of the nature of God (see vv. 4–11). Every believer has been given some gift (v. 7). Now the gifts are not primarily for building a place of worship, but to facilitate the construction of worship itself. So gifts such as wisdom, knowledge, preaching, prophesying and speaking in tongues ('different kinds of languages', v. 10) are mentioned, as well as performing miracles and healing the sick. The way in which these are to be evaluated, according to Paul, is the extent to which they help to build up the congregation (see 14:12, for instance). In line with this is how Paul indicates gifts such as speaking in tongues should be used. They are to be used in ways that facilitate the worship of the congregation and not merely to exalt the person with the gift; they are not for show but to show the reality of God within the gathered community.

How many gifts of the Spirit can you recognize being used in your worship services? Are you aware of the gifts of the Spirit that God has given to you? Are you able to rejoice in the richness of gifts that God has given to people in your church?

Prayer

Holy Spirit of God, help me to know if there are spiritual gifts that I find difficult to welcome. Help me to understand why this may be.

DS

Community-building: covenant renewed

I will wash away everything that makes you unclean, and I will remove your disgusting idols. I will take away your stubborn heart and give you a new heart and a desire to be faithful. You will have only pure thoughts, because I will put my Spirit in you and make you eager to obey my laws and teachings. You will once again live in the land I gave your ancestors; you will be my people, and I will be your God.

Yesterday's passage emphasized the importance of the Spirit for the worship of the community of God's people. Today's brings out an even more fundamental role of the Spirit within the life of God's people: only the Spirit can ensure the viability of the covenant people.

There is irony in this passage. God's punishment of Israel in the form of their exile to Babylon was intended to establish the holiness of God—Israel's blatant sins (murder and idolatry) had to be overtly punished. Rather than leading the Babylonians to recognize God's holiness, however, it had led to disgrace. They were saying that God had driven Israel out, turned against them and forsaken them (vv. 17–22). So God intends, even though they do not deserve it, to restore them to their land, re-establish his integrity. How can he do this and remain holy?

The pivotal answer is by means of his Spirit. All kinds of exciting promises precede this, such as bringing them home, cleansing them to make them acceptable to God, as well as removing their idols (vv. 24–25). All kinds of exhilarating promises follow, too, including ongoing protection from uncleanness, unprecedented prosperity, restoration of their towns and answered prayers (vv. 29–38), but at the core is the promise 'I will put my Spirit in you' (v. 27). He will make them eager to obey God's laws, they will have a new heart and so desire to be faithful. God will enable the covenant to be re-established and, with it, their identity and community: 'you will be my people, and I will be your God' (v. 28).

(If you have time, please read Jeremiah 31:31–34 and especially Ezekiel 36:17–38.)

Reflection

What does this passage have to say to a declining Church? Does it have anything to say to us as a nation?

DS

Community-building: covenant established

You Gentiles are no longer strangers and foreigners.... You are like a building with the apostles and prophets as the foundation and with Christ as the most important stone. Christ is the one who holds the building together and makes it grow into a holy temple for the Lord. And you are part of that building Christ has built as a place for God's own Spirit to live.

Paul never ceased to be amazed at the miracle of the death and resurrection of Jesus. Those who were enemies of God and dead to divine life, dead to their own destiny as people made in God's image and those who were intractable enemies of one another (the Jews and the Gentiles) had all been united as the people of God. Paul even dared to say that the Gentiles are part of the 'temple' along with the Jews. The temple was the most important place on earth for it was the place where heaven intersected with earth, being a symbol (perhaps we should say 'sacrament') of the place where God resides and makes his presence available. Paul knew the Gentiles were an integral part of God's new 'temple' because the Spirit of God lived among them too and there is only one Spirit (4:4).

This has moral and personal consequences. The Spirit of God is able to change the kinds of people we are and the ways we think and act, even as Ezekiel had predicted (see yesterday's reading). However, this only happens as we allow God's Spirit to operate in us. Hence, Paul writes, 'Try your best to let God's Spirit...' and 'Let the Spirit change your way of thinking...' (4:3 and 23). We are more involved than Ezekiel indicated as it takes effort to be humble, gentle and patient; it requires discipline to stop stealing, using dirty talk and cursing each other, if these have been our normal ways of living. However, if in this sense it's harder than Ezekiel thought, in another sense it is easier to know what pleasing God and being holy really means, for we have the life of Jesus as our focus and stimulus.

(Please read 4:3–4, 23–24, if you can.)

Prayer

Holy Spirit, do for us what we cannot and help us to be willing to let you.

DS

The Spirit and mission

The Spirit of the Lord God has taken control of me! The Lord has chosen and sent me to tell the oppressed the good news, to heal the brokenhearted, and to announce freedom for prisoners and captives. This is the year when the Lord God will show kindness to us and punish our enemies.

For all their familiarity, these verses still sound like a fanfare, demanding our attention and stirring hope in our hearts. They are even more startling because they are a personal claim, not one made to someone else. These verses tell of God's Spirit doing something new, although in one sense it is something old.

'Taking control' of someone is also the way the book of Judges (3:10; 6:34) describes the energizing intervention of God that enabled charismatic leaders to throw off the cruel domination of foreign tribes; yet here, in the context of exile and spiritual desolation, it is startlingly new.

Being 'chosen' by the Lord was what the coming of the Spirit indicated, but it also promised victory and favour. It became the word for Israel's king. Now that the monarchy was a forgotten reality or at best a historical reminiscence, to claim it as a present experience was revolutionary. The really startling claim was the purpose of the Spirit's coming—not primarily to destroy the enemy, but to commission a messenger to bring good news to the powerless and marginalized.

Here we see clearly the connection of God's Spirit with gospel mission, but there are two ways in which this amazing passage falls short of the New Testament's reality. First, the consequence of the realized hope for the oppressed is the destruction of Israel's enemies. Second, the focus of this outpouring of blessing is Jerusalem, not the whole world. True, foreigners do find a place, but only as hired labour, while the people of God become honoured as priests of God who receive all the treasures of the nations as tribute! Nevertheless, the fact that Jesus chose this passage to announce his ministry (Luke 4:18–19) suggests that we should value this passage very highly.

Meditation

Give yourself a spiritual check-up. Does your attitude to other people, groups and nations reflect the fuller revelation of the Spirit that Jesus gives?

DS

The Spirit and our mission

While he [Jesus] was still with them, he said: 'Don't leave Jerusalem yet. Wait here for the Father to give you the Holy Spirit, just as I told you he has promised to do… the Holy Spirit will come upon you and give you power. Then you will tell everyone about me in Jerusalem, in all Judea, in Samaria, and everywhere in the world.' … On the day of Pentecost all the Lord's followers were together in one place.

So the waiting was over and the time to move forward with the gospel of Jesus Christ had come. I try and imagine how those twelve disciples and the women with them would have felt.

Were they relieved that the waiting Jesus had prescribed was now over, as indeed was the perplexity about what exactly would happen when 'the Spirit comes upon you' and how they would know it had taken place. Were they even more confused by the outcome with so many people from so many cultures clamouring to join the Christian community (read on in chapter 2). The 120 believers were joined by another 5000. How would they cope with making them disciples? Surely there was no energy left to cope with expansion?

Were they excited beyond words as they experienced the 'greater things' that Jesus had promised would accompany the Spirit's coming? Were they fearful that such a movement of people into the Christian community, with all the ramifications for the Jewish leaders, would soon bring disaster on them?

I can only imagine how, had I had been one of them, all these reactions would have swept over me many times during those early days after Pentecost. One thing I would have known for sure, though — life could never be the same. God had pulled the cork out of the bottle and there was no way to get it back in again.

There is no way back. If we are impelled by the Holy Spirit, the Spirit of Jesus, we can only go forward, taking his offer of forgiveness, purpose, new identity, power to live by and hope to die for with us to share with all.

Meditation

Should we translate 'in Jerusalem, in all Judea, in Samaria, and everywhere in the world' (1:8) as family, friends, workmates and everyone with whom we have contact?

DS

Someone like me

He was despised and rejected by others; a man of suffering and acquainted with infirmity; and as one from whom others hide their faces he was despised, and we held him of no account. Surely he has borne our infirmities and carried our diseases; yet we accounted him stricken, struck down by God, and afflicted. But he was wounded for our transgressions, crushed for our iniquities; upon him was the punishment that made us whole, and by his bruises we are healed.

Last night I watched a programme on television about conjoined twins. It featured Russian sisters, with separate bodies but one pair of legs between them. They had been taken from their mother, raised in a brutal orphanage and are now alcoholics. They rarely go out, as people stare at them.

Their suffering is unimaginable. Yet, it's only one case in a world of suffering millions. Maybe it's because I'm going through treatment for cancer that I've chosen to start here, with an unnamed man who seems to have mysteriously taken on the pain of humankind. He, like those twins, 'had… nothing in his appearance that we should desire him' (v. 2)—the embarrassing outsider from whom others avert their eyes. He knew all about what it is to suffer physically and mentally.

This passage is, of course, taken by Christians as a prophecy of Christ. It is here the Ethiopian eunuch (Acts 8:26–35) famously started, and Philip from there 'proclaimed to him the good news about Jesus'. Here, too, evangelists to Jewish people, who have suffered so much, often start.

What this powerful poem says to me first of all is that there is no good news without an answer to the world's suffering. The answer, however, does not come in a neat argument; it comes as a person, a person like me, who's been through it all. 'It was fitting,' says the writer of Hebrews, 'that God… in bringing many children to glory, should make the pioneer of their salvation perfect [that is, complete] through sufferings' (Hebrews 2:10). Isaiah sums it up elsewhere: 'God with us' (7:14).

Reflection

'Son though he was, he learned obedience in the school of suffering' (Hebrews 5:8, NEB). What have you learned in that school?

VZ

A new world coming

For I am about to create new heavens and a new earth; the former things shall not be remembered or come to mind… I will rejoice in Jerusalem, and delight in my people; no more shall the sound of weeping be heard in it… No more shall there be in it an infant that lives but a few days, or an old person who does not live out a lifetime… They shall build houses and inhabit them; they shall plant vineyards and eat their fruit… The wolf and the lamb shall feed together, the lion shall eat straw like the ox… They shall not hurt or destroy on all my holy mountain.

I write as American and British fighter planes are bombing Kabul, in retaliation for the terrible attacks by terrorists in the US on 11 September 2001. It is hard to imagine how difficult this must be for the already starving and broken Afghan people, millions fleeing with nothing, seeking some kind of refuge. In the pain of this conflict, I turn again to Jesus' favourite prophet, Isaiah.

The vision of a new world is normally placed at the end of any explanation of the gospel, perhaps quoting the passage in Revelation 21, which echoes this one. I bring it in here, however, because I believe this hope of a true new world order, based not on politics or economics but on God's justice, is at the heart of the good news. If the answer to suffering comes as a person not an argument, we need also to know what that person stands for. It is an amazing vision, especially as it comes from so ancient a time, of a world where infant mortality is zero, the aged are not forced from their homes as refugees, peace and prosperity reign and even the animal kingdom is no longer 'red in tooth and claw'.

We must always remember, it is not 'God so loved *human beings* that he sent his only son…' but 'God so loved the *world*' (John 3:16). Jesus came, and comes, for the whole of creation around us, on which we depend.

Prayer

Bring before God a couple of places or situations in the world that concern you, then pray on their behalf: 'Come, Lord Jesus!' (Revelation 22:20).

VZ

Here I am

When he came to Nazareth, where he had been brought up, he went to the synagogue on the sabbath day, as was his custom. He stood up to read, and the scroll of the prophet Isaiah was given to him. He unrolled the scroll and found the place where it was written: 'The Spirit of the Lord is upon me, because he has anointed me to bring good news to the poor. He has sent me to proclaim release to the captives and recovery of sight to the blind, to let the oppressed go free, to proclaim the year of the Lord's favour.' ... Then he began to say to them, 'Today this scripture has been fulfilled in your hearing.'

Have you seen the newspaper adverts proclaiming that 'Maitreya, the Christ, is here'? It seems that few have believed this dramatic announcement of some new 'messiah' figure.

Few believed Jesus either (especially in his home town), but many have since! What is the difference that makes the difference? Jesus offered a test for true prophets: 'You will know them by their fruits' (Matthew 7:16). This test can be applied to Jesus himself; he not only quoted Isaiah, his own ministry prioritized the poor, the trapped, the disabled, the oppressed.

Jesus warned that, when he was no longer present in the flesh, others would come claiming 'I am he!' (Mark 13:6). So, it is vital that we learn to recognize the Spirit of the authentic Jesus. Only the one who proclaims 'good news to the poor' can say, 'Here I am; in the scroll of the book it is written of me' (Psalm 40:7) because he can also say the next verse, 'I delight to do your will, O my God' (40:8).

The same test can be applied to the Church. In so far as we pursue the acts of love and liberation that Jesus pursued, we are his true Church; in so far as we do not, we are not. When the Church be-comes an instrument of oppression (as it often, sadly, has), I suspect it has put something other than the man Jesus at the heart of its life. 'What would Jesus do?' can only be answered from the life of Jesus in the Gospels.

Prayer

'Teach me to do your will, for you are my God.'

Psalm 143:10

VZ

A new way of living

Now after John was arrested, Jesus came to Galilee, proclaiming the good news of God, and saying, 'The time is fulfilled, and the kingdom of God has come near; repent, and believe in the good news'.

Years before I was born, my mother answered the door to a stranger who announced baldly, 'I've come to rejoice with you.' He was, of course, a Christian wanting to share the good news of Jesus, but I can't help wondering what welcome he might have received had he come, say, to a house where someone had just died!

At the other end of the spectrum is the stock comic character who walks around with a sandwich board proclaiming, 'The end is nigh.' The trouble is, we seem to have difficulty balancing the good news of redemption with the bad news that we need redeeming. It's hard to see how 'repent' can be good news; yet that call is at the heart of the gospel.

Jesus doesn't seem to have had the same difficulty. Unlike many evangelists today, he didn't start with our sinfulness, he started with good news: the time is now, the Kingdom is near. For his hearers, who were waiting for a future golden age, that would make ears prick up. The Kingdom where the poor are rescued, the prisoners freed, the sick healed, the oppressed liberated, is right at hand, ready for us to reach out and grasp?

What response might we get if we started our proclamation of the gospel at that point today? Quite different, perhaps, than if we start by telling people that they have made a mess of things. Frankly, looking around at the world, I think people don't need much help to see that it's true.

We might, however, legitimately, be met with the question, 'How?' How is this ideal world of peace and justice to come about, human nature being what it is? That's where the second part of Jesus' announcement comes in: repent, literally 'change your minds'. This, too, is good news, not bad; for Jesus is telling us that this seemingly impossible demand is possible—with him.

Reflection

'And Jesus said to them, "Follow me…"' (Mark 1:17). Reflect on what this call has meant, and means, to you.

VZ

A new way of dying

So again Jesus said to them, 'Very truly, I tell you, I am the gate for the sheep... Whoever enters by me will be saved, and will come in and go out and find pasture... I am the good shepherd. The good shepherd lays down his life for the sheep... For this reason the Father loves me, because I lay down my life in order to take it up again. No one takes it from me, but I lay it down of my own accord... I have received this command from my Father.'

I'm sure some of you will be saying, 'Four readings already on the heart of the gospel, and she hasn't mentioned the cross yet!' Fair enough. For many, Jesus' death is their entry point into faith. Others may start elsewhere, as I did—encountering the personality of Jesus in the Gospels and feeling, 'Here is God'. This, after all, is where the first disciples started, before the cross had even happened. We may not discover the significance of Jesus' death until later.

However we start, I'm convinced that we can't understand Jesus' redeeming death without his redemptive life. The power of the cross comes from the cross-shaped life that led up to it. To 'lay down one's life' (John 15:13) is not just a single moment of death, but a whole life lived for others.

I don't understand fully how the cross 'works'. The Bible itself has many images: a religious sacrifice for sins; a legal punishment taken on by another; God joining in our own weakness and suffering; death defeated by the power of love. It is a mystery, and it will always yield new depths.

All I know is that here I see God 'on my side'; not in the narrow sense of endorsing all I think and do, but in a love that is deep enough to cancel all my failings. 'Perhaps for a good person someone might actually dare to die. But God proves his love for us in that while we were still sinners Christ died for us' (Romans 5:7–8). That, in the end, is what makes Jesus unique.

Reflection

Tis mystery all! The Immortal dies: Who can explore his strange design?

...Tis mercy all! let earth adore, Let angel minds inquire no more.

Charles Wesley, 1707–88
VZ

A new kind of freedom

Do you not know that all of us who have been baptized into Christ Jesus were baptized into his death? Therefore we have been buried with him by baptism into death, so that, just as Christ was raised from the dead by the glory of the Father, so we too might walk in newness of life... But thanks be to God that you, having once been slaves of sin, have become obedient from the heart to the form of teaching to which you were entrusted, and that you, having been set free from sin, have become slaves of righteousness.

Do you remember the television series *The Fall and Rise of Reginald Perrin*? It centred on a character who faked his own death to start a new life. It's a common fantasy: just leave everything behind and reinvent ourselves, free of ties, making none of the mistakes we made before.

Few actually do it, and if we did we would soon acquire new complications and failures. There is, however, another way of 'dying' and starting again.

I remember at my baptism, as a teenager, coming up out of the water and thinking, 'Now I have started a new life.' It was not that I never did wrong again—indeed, my struggle for Christ-likeness was just beginning —but the act proclaimed symbolically that I was now 'in Christ'; his death and resurrection were re-enacted in me. One person went under the water, a different person came out. I wasn't a person free of ties— I still had duties to my parents,

friends and the world around me. Now, though, they were all secondary to a greater commitment, one the implications of which would take a lifetime to work out.

'A Christian is a perfectly free lord of all, subject to none. A Christian is a perfectly dutiful servant of all, subject to all' (Martin Luther). This is the paradox of serving Christ: it is the yoke that fits us (Matthew 11:29), the burden that, unlike most, becomes lighter the longer we carry it.

Reflection

'For freedom Christ has set us free. Stand firm, therefore, and do not submit again to a yoke of slavery' (Galatians 5:1).
What kinds of 'slavery' threaten you: habit, tradition, other people's opinions? How is Christ offering to set you free?

VZ

A new community

When Jesus saw the crowds, he went up the mountain... and taught them, saying: 'Blessed are the poor in spirit, for theirs is the kingdom of heaven. Blessed are those who mourn, for they will be comforted. Blessed are the meek, for they will inherit the earth. Blessed are those who hunger and thirst for righteousness, for they will be filled. Blessed are the merciful, for they will receive mercy. Blessed are the pure in heart, for they will see God. Blessed are the peacemakers, for they will be called children of God. Blessed are those who are persecuted for righteousness' sake, for theirs is the kingdom of heaven.'

It was a liberating insight when I heard a preacher say that this is not a set of commands, but a description of a community. We needn't strive to be poor in spirit, to be meek, to mourn. This is simply what the 'Jesus-shaped' Church looks like. The Church is not a power base, a campaign, a 'ministry for the promotion of virtue and suppression of vice'. It is a community of the weak, the failures, those who long for themselves and their world to be better and weep that they and it are not.

When I saw that students at a theology college were set an essay to be entitled 'What are we saved from?' I wanted to rewrite the question as 'What are we saved for?' Christ rescues us from our worst selves to build us into a city on a hill (Matthew 5.14), a new model of living.

We are back where we started, with a mysterious way of bringing redemption out of suffering; with a Kingdom that starts as small as a mustard seed and grows into a whole new world. We started with Isaiah's prophecy of Christ the person. We end with 'Christ the people'—the mind-blowing idea that we, together, are his body, making his words flesh in our lives, even in our wounds. The Spirit of the Lord is upon us now. That's what I call the 'full gospel'.

Reflection

'And all of us... seeing the glory of the Lord as though reflected in a mirror, are being transformed into the same image from one degree of glory to another' (2 Corinthians 3:18). *Savour this picture; enjoy God's glory.*

VZ

Wisdom to choose

To what then will I compare the people of this generation, and what are they like? They are like children sitting in the marketplace and calling to one another, 'We played the flute for you, and you did not dance; we wailed, and you did not weep.' For John the Baptist has come eating no bread and drinking no wine, and you say, 'He has a demon'; the Son of Man has come eating and drinking, and you say, 'Look, a glutton and a drunkard, a friend of tax-collectors and sinners!' Nevertheless, wisdom is vindicated by all her children.

'Some people are never satisfied', you can almost hear Jesus say in exasperation. He has just healed the centurion's slave, and the widow of Nain's son. He has named John the Baptist as a great prophet and God's messenger, preparing the way for the Messiah. Yet, many of the religious people, the Pharisees and the lawyers, refuse to accept either John or Jesus. They are, says Jesus, like spoilt, sulky children, who won't join in with the game their friends are playing, because it's always the wrong game.

So, John comes, living an ascetic life, living in the wilderness and fasting, and they accuse him of being possessed. Jesus comes, eating and drinking, often with the less respectable people, and they accuse him of being a greedy drunkard. God, though, has sent both John and Jesus. Each is honouring God in the way he lives, and each has his own followers.

Certainly Jesus had fasted and would fast again, but, for now, it was right to feast, to share meals with those who were not usually invited to feasts. John's ministry and Jesus' ministry complement each other, yet each is criticized for not doing what the other does.

'For everything there is a season… a time to mourn, and a time to dance' (Ecclesiastes 3:1, 4). We need the wisdom to know what is right for this season and time. Jesus, the wisdom of God (1 Corinthians 1:24), leads his children so we know when it is time to fast or to feast, to mourn or to dance.

Reflection

Jesus, wisdom of God, make me sensitive to your leading and ready to follow wholeheartedly.

HJ CSF

Generous God

Ho, everyone who thirsts, come to the waters; and you that have no money, come, buy and eat! Come, buy wine and milk without money and without price. Why do you spend your money for that which is not bread, and your labour for that which does not satisfy? Listen carefully to me, and eat what is good, and delight yourselves in rich food. Incline your ear, and come to me; listen, so that you may live.

Visiting India, I was struck by the number of people selling water by the roadside. A very small sum bought a glass of water, with a squeeze of lime. Imagine having to buy your water by the glassful or, even worse, being too poor to pay even the tiny price of a drink? Especially in a hot country, that really is being in want.

In this parable, God is a water seller like no other. The familiar cry, drawing attention to what he has to sell, is transformed. This water seller is giving away his stock free to anyone who needs it. His stock is not only water, but also bread, and not only bread and water, the necessities of life, but also wine and milk, the luxuries.

In Isaiah's parable, God is not only the street seller, but also the rich benefactor. Someone wishing to be generous would buy up the entire stock of a water-carrier or a baker and order him to distribute it free. God does this not once but continuously. His generosity is unmatched.

There is still more. Not content with supplying free both the necessities of life and the luxuries, he goes on to promise the gift of life itself. Bread and water, wine and milk, may be necessary and pleasurable, but they are not enough. If all our energies are focused on them and what they stand for, we will ultimately not be satisfied. Only in coming to God and listening to his word—the Word, Jesus—will we receive the greatest gift of our generous God: 'I came that they may have life, and have it abundantly' (John 10:10).

Reflection

On what do I spend my money and my labour?

HJ CSF

Show me

Blow the trumpet in Zion; sound the alarm on my holy mountain! Let all the inhabitants of the land tremble, for the day of the Lord is coming, it is near… a great and powerful army comes… Yet even now, says the Lord, return to me with all your heart, with fasting, with weeping, and with mourning; rend your hearts and not your clothing. Return to the Lord, your God, for he is gracious and merciful, slow to anger, and abounding in steadfast love, and relents from punishing. Who knows whether he will not turn and relent, and leave a blessing behind him, a grain offering and a drink offering for the Lord, your God?

'Don't talk of love, show me,' sang Eliza Doolittle in *My Fair Lady*. Here are God's people, facing a great calamity, a mighty army advancing on them, and this is God's doing—'the day of the Lord is coming'. Recognizing this, the people want to demonstrate to God their sorrow for their sins, their unfaithfulness, everything that has brought this day on them. Just talking about it won't do. Like Eliza Doolittle, God wants something more concrete. Fasting and weeping and mourning are ways of showing God their love and sorrow. They back up the words and strengthen them.

But even such dramatic action, though more effective than words alone, is not enough. The call is to repent 'with all your heart'. For the Hebrews, this did not necessarily mean 'with all your feeling'. The heart represented intellect and will as much as emotions, so perhaps 'with all your heart' could be translated as 'with purpose and resolve'. The heart must also be torn, broken, as mourners tore their clothes as a sign of grief.

The heart, broken open, with a real resolution to change, can then truly turn, return, repent and come back into a relationship with the gracious and merciful God. This return is celebrated with feasting, grain and drink offerings to God, who waits with steadfast love to feast with his people.

Reflection

What authentic ways can I find of showing God my penitence for sin?

HJ CSF

Glory to God

And whenever you fast, do not look dismal, like the hypocrites, for they disfigure their faces so as to show others that they are fasting. Truly I tell you, they have received their reward. But when you fast, put oil on your head and wash your face, so that your fasting may be seen not by others but by your Father who is in secret; and your Father who sees in secret will reward you.

The key word here is 'whenever'. Jesus takes it for granted that his disciples will give alms, pray and fast and here he tells them how to go about these practices. 'How to' is only the beginning, though—far more important, and far more demanding, is 'why'.

'Beware of practising your piety before others in order to be seen by them…' (6:1). The almsgiver should not be accompanied down the street by a servant blowing a trumpet. The one who prays should go into their room and shut the door. When Jesus' disciples fast, it should be as a personal act of devotion between them and God. No one else should be able to tell. They should look and act as they normally do.

Does this contradict what Jesus said just a little earlier in the Sermon on the Mount—'Let your light shine before others, so that they may see your good works' (5:16)? No, because, again, the motivation is all-important. Verse 16 goes on to say 'and give glory to your Father in heaven'. God must be the focus of almsgiving, prayer and fasting and God's reward is the only one the disciples long for. It's a good test of our Lent resolutions this Ash Wednesday.

Our natural human tendency to want others to think well of us is a problem for the spiritual life. It makes us self-conscious, aware of being seen. The great saints, Francis among them, seem to have escaped this. Francis responded directly to God, praying, singing, dancing, weeping, fasting or feasting. He was so intoxicated with God that he was oblivious of others' opinions of him. His eyes were fixed on God and God's was all the glory.

Prayer

God of glory, help me to fix my eyes only on you.

HJ CSF

Hungry for God

There was also a prophet, Anna the daughter of Phanuel, of the tribe of Asher. She was of a great age, having lived with her husband for seven years after her marriage, then as a widow to the age of 84. She never left the temple but worshipped there with fasting and prayer night and day. At that moment she came, and began to praise God and to speak about the child to all who were looking for the redemption of Jerusalem.

'She's never out of the church' may be a compliment or rather less than one. We may perhaps think of a lonely old woman, with no life of her own. Anna, however, who 'never left the temple', is not one of those.

Only seven women in the whole of the Old Testament are named as prophets. Anna's long life of worship in the temple in Jerusalem—the centre of the world for God's people—made her especially sensitive to the signs of God's presence. Like Simeon, she had waited faithfully for the coming of the Messiah. So, when the child Jesus was brought into the temple, she recognized him and knew that this was cause for rejoicing.

Her worship included both prayer and fasting and, in the scriptures, these two usually belong together. Fasting from food in order to focus more completely on God has a long pedigree. Of course, it isn't automatically successful. I have a friend who became so desperate for chocolate while on a fasting retreat that he walked eight miles over mountain paths to buy a bar. 'It was all that was good in the universe,' he recalled. Fasting is not an automatic passport to opening up in us a hunger for God. Rather, it may make it humiliatingly clear where our hunger really lies.

Perhaps Anna, too, found it hard in the beginning. However, she persevered, perhaps for as long as 60 years, and, in the end, her hunger was satisfied. Like Simeon, her eyes saw God's salvation and her soul rejoiced.

Reflection

What am I hungry for?
How might fasting, from food or something else, help me to focus more on God this Lent?

HJ CSF

True fasting

Is not this the fast that I choose: to loose the bonds of injustice, to undo the thongs of the yoke, to let the oppressed go free, and to break every yoke? Is it not to share your bread with the hungry, and bring the homeless poor into your house; when you see the naked, to cover them, and not to hide yourself from your own kin? Then your light shall break forth like the dawn, and your healing shall spring up quickly.

My mother recalls that my sister and I would burst in from school saying, 'Do you know, it's not fair', before we'd even taken our coats off. Then would follow some saga of injustice. The instinct for fair play is a very deep one.

God's people think that he isn't treating them fairly. Just before this passage, they are complaining, 'Why do we fast, but you do not see? Why humble ourselves, but you do not notice?' (v. 3). We are doing all the right things, God. Why are you not rewarding us as we deserve?

God's reply is devastating. Your fasting is worthless if it is accompanied by oppression, quarrelling and violence (vv. 3–4). Fasting like this is only an outward show, an empty ritual.

Then God details what must accompany fasting if it is to be pleasing to him. Justice, liberation, compassion and care for neighbour are what God chooses. These are what please him, these are what will cause him to hear his people when they call to him.

The prophets call their hearers to 'do justice, and to love kindness' (Micah 6:8). God cares passionately about justice, but we cannot bargain our way into his favour with our fasting or our beautiful services or our long prayers. These have their place, but God looks for justice and compassion, expressed in the very concrete details of our lives, as well.

Prayer

Merciful God, you loose the bonds of injustice and let the oppressed go free: give us the will to share our bread with the hungry and give shelter to the homeless poor, for thus your glory shall be revealed, through Jesus Christ our Lord. Amen

HJ CSF

The feast of the Kingdom

He said also to the one who had invited him, 'When you give a luncheon or a dinner, do not invite your friends or your brothers or your relatives or rich neighbours, in case they may invite you in return, and you would be repaid. But when you give a banquet, invite the poor, the crippled, the lame, and the blind. And you will be blessed, because they cannot repay you, for you will be repaid at the resurrection of the righteous.'

When I moved to the East End of London, I knew what kind of church I wanted to join. I would look for somewhere fairly large and successful where, for a time, I could just sidle in and out and not be asked to do anything. I ended up in a tiny congregation, at that time without a priest, where I was immediately pressed into service, but in the end I was grateful.

Although small, the congregation came from an amazing range of backgrounds. On an average Sunday, there would be traditional working-class East Enders, a retired teacher or two from the leafier suburbs, me from Scotland, two or three older people from the Caribbean, a young family from the Far East, perhaps a Latin American. The priest who soon came to care for the parish was Anglo-Indian. I used to look around at the Eucharist and think, 'This is what the Kingdom looks like.' People from all classes and ages and all parts of the world, united by nothing at all except their desire to worship God.

This is one of Jesus' parables of the Kingdom. The feast of the Kingdom is not like most of our parties—a time to enjoy our friends or perhaps impress our neighbours or colleagues, knowing that next it will be their turn to invite us. The feast of the Kingdom is, as theological commentator Dennis McBride says, for 'people who need food because they are hungry, who need company because they are outcast, who need rejoicing because they know sadness, who need sharing because they are isolated in their sickness'.

Reflection

What would it mean in my life and in my church to follow Jesus' advice to his host?

HJ CSF

ALSO PUBLISHED BY BRF

GUIDELINES

Guidelines is a unique Bible reading resource that offers four months of in-depth study written by leading scholars. Contributors are drawn from around the world, as well as the UK, and represent a thought-provoking breadth of Christian tradition. Instead of dated readings, *Guidelines* provides weekly units, broken into six sections, plus an introduction and a final section of points for thought and prayer. On any day you can read as many or as few sections as you wish. As well as a copy of *Guidelines*, you will need a Bible, as the passage is not included.

DAY BY DAY WITH GOD

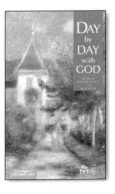

Day by Day with God (published jointly with Christina Press) is written especially by women for women, with a regular team of contributors. Each four-monthly issue offers daily Bible readings, with key verses printed out, helpful comment and a prayer for the day ahead.

HOW TO ORDER BRF NOTES

If you have enjoyed reading this sampler and would like to order the dated notes on a regular basis, they can be obtained through:

CHRISTIAN BOOKSHOPS

Most Christian bookshops stock BRF notes and books. You can place a regular order with your bookshop for yourself or for your church. For details of your nearest stockist please contact the BRF office.

INDIVIDUAL SUBSCRIPTION

For yourself

By placing an annual subscription for BRF notes, you can ensure you will receive your copy regularly. We also send you additional information about BRF: BRF News, information about our new publications and updates about our ministry activities.

You can also order a subscription for three years (two years for *Day by Day with God*), for an even easier and more economical way to obtain your Bible reading notes.

Gift subscription

Why not give a gift subscription to *New Daylight*, *Guidelines* or *Day by Day with God* to a friend or family member? Simply complete all parts of the order form on the next page and return it to us with your payment. You can even enclose a message for the gift recipient.

For either of the above, please complete the 'Individual Subscription Order Form' and send with your payment to BRF.

CHURCH SUBSCRIPTION

If you order, directly from BRF, five or more copies from our Bible reading notes range of *New Daylight*, *Guidelines* or *Day by Day with God*, they will be sent post-free. This is known as a church subscription and it is a convenient way of bulk-ordering notes for your church. There is no need to send payment with your initial order. Please complete the 'Church Subscriptions Order Form' and we will send you an invoice with your first delivery of notes.

- **Annual subscription:** you can place a subscription for a full year, receiving one invoice for the year. Once you place an annual church subscription, you will be sent the requested number of Bible reading notes automatically. You will also receive useful information to help you run your church group. You can amend your order at any time, as your requirements increase or decrease. Church subscriptions run from May to April of each year. If you start in the middle of a subscription year, you will receive an invoice for the remaining issues of the current subscription year.

- **Standing order:** we can set up a standing order for your Bible reading notes order. Approximately six to seven weeks before a new edition of the notes is due to start, we will process your order and send it with an invoice.

CHURCH SUBSCRIPTIONS

Name _____

Address _____

_____

_____ Postcode _____

Telephone Number_____

E-mail _____

Church _____

Denomination _____

Name of Minister _____

Please start my order from Jan/May/Sep* *(delete as applicable)*

I would like to pay annually / receive an invoice each issue of the notes
(delete as applicable)

Please send me: **Quantity**

New Daylight   _____

New Daylight Large Print   _____

Guidelines   _____

Day by Day with God   _____

Please do not enclose payment. We have a fixed subscription year for Church Subscriptions, which is from May to April each year. If you start a Church Subscription in the middle of a subscription year, we will invoice you for the number of issues remaining in that year.

INDIVIDUAL & GIFT SUBSCRIPTIONS

☐ I would like to give a gift subscription (please complete both name and address sections below)

☐ I would like to take out a subscription myself (complete name and address details only once)

This completed coupon should be sent with appropriate payment to BRF. Alternatively, please write to us quoting your name, address, the subscription you would like for either yourself or a friend (with their name and address), the start date and credit card number, expiry date and signature if paying by credit card.

Gift subscription name _____

Gift subscription address _____

_____

_____ Postcode _____

Please send beginning with the May / September / January issue: *(delete as applicable)*

(please tick box)	**UK**	**SURFACE**	**AIR MAIL**
New Daylight	☐ £11.10	☐ £12.45	☐ £14.70
New Daylight 3-year sub	☐ £27.45		
New Daylight LARGE PRINT	☐ £16.80	☐ £20.40	☐ £24.90
Guidelines	☐ £11.10	☐ £12.45	☐ £14.70
Guidelines 3-year sub	☐ £27.45		
Day by Day with God	☐ £12.15	☐ £13.50	☐ £15.75
Day by Day with God 2-year sub	☐ £20.40		

Please complete the payment details below and send your coupon, with appropriate payment to: BRF, First Floor, Elsfield Hall, 15–17 Elsfield Way, Oxford OX2 8FG.

Your name _____

Your address _____

_____

_____ Postcode _____

Total enclosed £ _____ (cheques should be made payable to 'BRF')

Payment by ☐ cheque ☐ postal order ☐ Visa ☐ Mastercard ☐ Switch

Card number: ☐☐☐☐☐☐☐☐☐☐☐☐☐☐☐☐☐☐

Expiry date of card: ☐☐☐☐   Issue number (Switch): ☐☐☐

Signature _____ Date /   /
(essential if paying by credit/Switch card)

NDSAM03   *BRF is a Registered Charity*